U.S. Department of Justice

Office of Justice Programs

Office of Juvenile Justice and Delinquency Prevention

Juvenile Offenders and Victims:

National

Report Series

Bulletin

September 2013

Juvenile Residential Facility Census, 2010: Selected Findings

Sarah Hockenberry, Melissa Sickmund, and Anthony Sladky

A Message From OJJDP

The Office of Juvenile Justice and Delinquency Prevention's biennial Juvenile Residential Facility Census (JRFC) collects information about facilities in which juvenile offenders are held. Respondents provide information about facility characteristics, including facility type, capacity, and type of security. JRFC also reports the number of youth who were injured or died in custody during the past 12 months.

This bulletin provides findings from the 2010 survey. The juvenile offender population dropped 18% from 2008 to 2010. Issues of crowding and overcapacity at these facilities, however, continue to be of concern. In 2010, about 18% of facilities were at their standard bed capacity, and 2% were over capacity.

The 2010 JRFC data also describe the range of services that facilities provide to youth in their care. Almost all facilities (92%) reported that a portion of or all residents attended some type of schooling. Most responding facilities routinely evaluated all juvenile offenders for substance use (70%), mental health needs (57%), and suicide risk (89%).

Together, JRFC and its companion survey, the Census of Juveniles in Residential Placement, which describes the demographics of youth in custody, allow the corrections community, juvenile justice professionals, youth advocates, and policymakers to monitor conditions of confinement and ensure that the nation's juvenile residential facilities are safe and that youth in custody receive the necessary treatment and services.

Robert L. Listenbee
Administrator

The Juvenile Residential Facility Census provides data on facility operations

Facility census describes 2,519 juvenile facilities

In October 2010, the Office of Juvenile Justice and Delinquency Prevention (OJJDP) administered the sixth Juvenile Residential Facility Census (JRFC). JRFC began in 2000 with data collections occurring every other year.

JRFC routinely collects data on how facilities operate and the services they provide. It includes detailed questions on facility security, capacity and crowding, injuries and deaths in custody, and facility ownership and operation. Supplementary information is also collected each year on specific services, such as mental and physical health, substance abuse, and education.

JRFC does not capture data on adult prisons or jails, nor does it include facilities used exclusively for mental health or substance abuse treatment or for dependent children. Thus, JRFC includes most, but not all, facilities that hold juvenile offenders. The reporting facilities may also hold adults or "nonoffenders," but data were only included if the facility held at least one juvenile offender on the census date.

The 2010 JRFC collected data from 2,519 juvenile facilities. Analyses in this bulletin were based on data from 2,111 facilities, which held a total of 66,322 offenders younger than 21 on the census date (October 27, 2010). JRFC excluded data from 6 facilities in Puerto Rico and the Virgin Islands, 19 tribal facilities, and 383 facilities that held no juvenile offenders on that date.

JRFC is one component in a multitiered effort to describe the youth placed in residential facilities and the facilities themselves. Other components include:

- **The National Juvenile Court Data Archive,** which collects information on sanctions that juvenile courts impose.

- **The Census of Juveniles in Residential Placement,** which collects information on the demographics and legal attributes of each youth in a juvenile facility on the census date.

- **The Survey of Youth in Residential Placement,** which collected a broad range of self-reported information from interviews in 2003 with individual youth in residential placement.

On October 27, 2010, 51% of juvenile facilities were publicly operated; they held 70% of juvenile offenders

State	Juvenile facilities			Juvenile offenders			State	Juvenile facilities			Juvenile offenders		
	Total	Public	Private	Total	Public	Private		Total	Public	Private	Total	Public	Private
U.S. total	2,111	1,074	1,037	66,322	46,677	19,645	Missouri	64	60	4	1,237	1,168	69
Alabama	49	13	36	1,059	504	555	Montana	13	8	5	153	130	23
Alaska	19	8	11	274	216	58	Nebraska	12	5	7	680	412	268
Arizona	33	15	18	1,398	947	451	Nevada	22	13	9	875	676	199
Arkansas	33	11	22	748	260	488	New Hampshire	7	2	5	130	64	66
California	202	109	93	10,908	9,781	1,127	New Jersey	39	34	5	1,209	1,178	31
Colorado	44	13	31	1,367	819	548	New Mexico	21	15	6	504	458	46
Connecticut	10	4	6	286	216	70	New York	126	31	95	2,356	1,005	1,351
Delaware	7	6	1	208	195	13	North Carolina	41	24	17	824	577	247
Dist. of Columbia	9	2	7	250	196	54	North Dakota	13	4	9	193	76	117
Florida	97	34	63	4,526	1,565	2,961	Ohio	77	63	14	2,683	2,508	175
Georgia	33	25	8	2,055	1,694	361	Oklahoma	35	15	20	698	460	238
Hawaii	5	3	2	86	79	7	Oregon	44	23	21	1,267	1,009	258
Idaho	20	14	6	477	411	66	Pennsylvania	131	29	102	4,403	1,012	3,391
Illinois	40	27	13	2,161	1,949	212	Rhode Island	11	1	10	292	144	148
Indiana	70	34	36	1,968	1,275	693	South Carolina	21	8	13	864	556	308
Iowa	63	14	49	989	298	691	South Dakota	21	8	13	426	228	198
Kansas	34	16	18	889	695	194	Tennessee	38	26	12	884	675	209
Kentucky	33	28	5	851	806	45	Texas	97	82	15	4,916	4,451	465
Louisiana	34	17	17	1,087	837	250	Utah	28	16	12	637	383	254
Maine	4	2	2	185	181	4	Vermont	3	1	2	26	13	13
Maryland	30	14	16	892	702	190	Virginia	52	49	3	1,759	1,709	50
Massachusetts	52	19	33	694	261	433	Washington	34	31	3	1,182	1,134	48
Michigan	62	30	32	1,793	939	854	West Virginia	26	11	15	467	341	126
Minnesota	54	22	32	955	585	370	Wisconsin	66	20	46	1,077	583	494
Mississippi	16	13	3	243	211	32	Wyoming	16	2	14	231	105	126

Notes: "State" is the state where the facility is located. Offenders sent to out-of-state facilities are counted in the state where the facility is located, not the state where they committed their offense. Data collected from 6 facilities in Puerto Rico and the Virgin Islands and 19 tribal facilities are not included.

Source: Authors' analysis of *Juvenile Residential Facility Census 2010* [machine-readable data file].

Although most facilities were small and private, most offenders were held in large public facilities

Local facilities were more numerous, but state facilities held as many offenders

Historically, local facilities (those staffed by county, city, or municipal employees) held fewer juvenile offenders than state facilities, despite accounting for more than half of all public facilities. In recent years the gap narrowed and, in 2010, local and state facilities held the same amount of offenders.

	Facilities		Juvenile offenders	
	Number	Percent	Number	Percent
Total	2,111	100%	66,322	100%
Public	1,074	51	46,677	70
State	440	21	23,237	35
Local	634	30	23,440	35
Private	1,037	49	19,645	30

Note: Detail may not total 100% because of rounding.

In 2010, JRFC asked facilities if a for-profit agency owned and/or operated them. Of reporting facilities, only a small percentage said that these types of agencies owned (4%) or operated (7%) them. In both cases, these facilities tended to hold 100 or fewer residents and were most likely to classify themselves as residential treatment centers.

Residential treatment centers and group homes outnumbered other types of facilities

JRFC asks respondents to identify the type of facility (e.g., detention center, shelter, reception/diagnostic center, group home/halfway house, boot camp, ranch/forestry/wilderness camp/marine program, training school/long-term secure facility, or residential treatment center). JRFC allowed respondents to select more

Training schools tend to be state facilities, detention centers tend to be local facilities, and group homes tend to be private facilities

	Facility type							
Facility operation	Total	Detention center	Shelter	Reception/ diagnostic center	Group home	Ranch/ wilderness camp	Training school	Residential treatment center
Number of facilities	2,111	705	137	72	528	68	188	763
Operations profile								
All facilities	100%	100%	100%	100%	100%	100%	100%	100%
Public	51	87	35	69	18	47	91	34
State	21	20	3	57	10	9	80	18
Local	30	67	32	13	9	38	11	15
Private	49	13	65	31	82	53	9	66
Facility profile								
All facilities	100%	33%	6%	3%	25%	3%	9%	36%
Public	100	57	4	5	9	3	16	24
State	100	33	1	9	12	1	34	32
Local	100	74	7	1	7	4	3	18
Private	100	9	9	2	42	3	2	49

- Detention centers, reception/diagnostic centers, and training schools were more likely to be public facilities than private facilities; however, a substantial proportion of reception/diagnostic centers were private.
- Most shelters were private facilities, as were group homes and residential treatment centers.
- Detention centers made up the largest proportion of all local facilities and more than half of all public facilities.
- Training schools constituted 34% of all state facilities.
- Group homes accounted for 42% of all private facilities.

Note: Counts (and row percentages) may sum to more than the total number of facilities because facilities could select more than one facility type.

Source: Authors' analysis of *Juvenile Residential Facility Census 2010* [machine-readable data file].

than one facility type, although the vast majority (85%) selected only one.

Slightly more than 760 facilities identified themselves as residential treatment centers and were holding juvenile offenders on the 2010 census date. Residential treatment centers made up 36% of all facilities and held 36% of juvenile offenders. Nearly 530 facilities identified themselves as group homes/halfway houses and were holding juvenile offenders. Group homes made up 25% of facilities and held 10% of juvenile offenders. There were 109 facilities that identified

themselves as both residential treatment centers and group homes. In fact, the group home/residential treatment center combination was the most common facility type combination. There were 705 facilities that identified themselves as detention centers—they accounted for 33% of facilities and held 41% of juvenile offenders in residential placement on the census date. Facilities identified as detention centers most commonly also identified themselves as residential treatment centers (64 facilities), training schools (35), and reception/diagnostic centers (22).

Security features and size varied across types of facilities

Facilities varied in their degree of security

Overall, 43% of facilities said that, at least some of the time, they locked youth in their sleeping rooms. Among public facilities, 78% of local facilities and 64% of state facilities reported locking youth in sleeping rooms. Few private facilities locked youth in sleeping rooms (9%).

Percentage of facilities locking youth in sleeping rooms

Total	43%
Public	72
State	64
Local	78
Private	9

Note: Percentages are based on facilities that reported security information (152 of 2,111 facilities [7%] did not report).

Among facilities that locked youth in sleeping rooms, most did this at night (85%) or when a youth was out of control (79%). Locking doors whenever youth were in their sleeping rooms (59%) and locking youth in their rooms during shift changes (50%) were also fairly common. Fewer facilities reported locking youth in sleeping rooms for a part of each day (28%) or when they were suicidal (26%). Very few facilities locked youth in sleeping rooms most of each day (2%) or all of each day (less than 1%). Seven percent (7%) had no set schedule for locking youth in sleeping rooms.

Facilities indicated whether they had various types of locked doors or gates intended to confine youth within the facility (see sidebar, this page). More than half of all facilities that reported security information said they had one or more confinement features (other than locked sleeping rooms). A greater proportion of public facilities (84%) than private facilities (26%) had confinement features.

Percentage of facilities

	No confinement features	One or more confinement features
Total	43%	57%
Public	16	84
State	15	85
Local	16	84
Private	74	26

Note: Percentages are based on facilities that reported security information (152 of 2,111 facilities [7%] did not report).

Among detention centers and training schools that reported security information, more than 9 in 10 said they had one or more confinement features (other than locked sleeping rooms).

Facilities reporting one or more confinement features (other than locked sleeping rooms):

Facility type	Number	Percentage
Total facilities	1,113	57%
Detention center	642	95
Shelter	33	25
Reception/diagnostic center	55	79
Group home	76	16
Ranch/wilderness camp	17	29
Training school	167	96
Residential treatment center	338	48

Note: Detail sums to more than totals because facilities could select more than one facility type.

Among group homes, fewer than 1 in 5 facilities said they had locked doors or gates to confine youth. A facility's staff, of course, also provides security. In some facilities, a remote location is a security feature that also helps to keep youth from leaving.

Overall, 23% of facilities reported external gates in fences or walls with razor wire. This arrangement was most common among training schools (46%), detention centers (45%), and reception/diagnostic centers (36%).

Security increased as facility size increased

Among the largest facilities (those with more than 200 residents) that provided security information, 74% locked youth in their sleeping rooms to confine them at least some of the time. The vast majority of large facilities (80%) had one or more features (locked doors or gates) intended to confine youth.

| | Percentage of facilities reporting | | |
Facility size	Youth locked in sleep rooms	One or more confinement features	Razor wire
Total facilities	43%	57%	23%
1–10 residents	22	31	7
11–20 residents	39	55	20
21–50 residents	55	71	30
51–100 residents	60	82	42
101–200 residents	75	85	43
201+ residents	74	80	60

Although the use of razor wire is a far less common security measure, 6 in 10 of the largest facilities said they had locked gates in fences or walls with razor wire.

Large facilities were most likely to be state operated

Few (13%) state-operated facilities (58 of 440) held 10 or fewer residents in 2010. In contrast, 45% of private facilities (468 of 1,037) were that small. In fact, these small private facilities made up the largest proportion of private facilities.

| | Facility operation | | |
Facility size	State	Local	Private
Total facilities	440	634	1,037
1–10 residents	58	150	468
11–20 residents	95	152	234
21–50 residents	142	203	218
51–100 residents	71	89	83
101–200 residents	57	28	23
201+ residents	17	12	11

More than half of facilities were small (holding 20 or fewer residents), although nearly half of juvenile offenders were held in medium facilities (holding 21–100 residents)

Facility size	Number of facilities	Percentage of facilities	Number of juvenile offenders	Percentage of juvenile offenders
Total facilities	2,111	100%	66,322	100%
1–10 residents	676	32	3,500	5
11–20 residents	481	23	6,220	9
21–50 residents	563	27	16,340	25
51–100 residents	243	12	15,705	24
101–200 residents	108	5	13,928	21
201+ residents	40	2	10,629	16

■ Although the largest facilities—those holding more than 200 residents—accounted for only 2% of all facilities, they held 16% of all juvenile offenders in custody.

■ Inversely, although the smallest facilities—those holding 10 or fewer residents— accounted for 32% of all facilities, they held only 5% of all juvenile offenders in custody.

Note: Column percentages may not add up to 100% due to rounding.

Source: Authors' analysis of *Juvenile Residential Facility Census 2010* [machine-readable data file].

Small group homes holding 20 or fewer residents were the most common type of facility

| | Facility type | | | | | | |
Facility size	Detention center	Shelter	Reception/ diagnostic center	Group home	Ranch/ wilderness camp	Training school	Residential treatment center
Number of facilities	705	137	72	528	68	188	763
Total facilities	100%	100%	100%	100%	100%	100%	100%
1–10 residents	22	53	11	65	7	3	20
11–20 residents	24	28	17	18	19	11	25
21–50 residents	34	14	28	12	40	29	33
51–100 residents	13	3	21	3	25	24	15
101–200 residents	6	1	17	1	6	23	4
201+ residents	3	1	7	1	3	10	2

■ 65% of group homes and 53% of shelters held 10 or fewer residents. For other facility types, this proportion was less than 23%.

■ 10% of training schools and 7% of reception/diagnostic centers held more than 200 residents. For other facility types, this proportion was less than 4%.

Note: Facility type counts sum to more than 2,111 facilities because facilities could select more than one facility type. Column percentages may not add up to 100% due to rounding.

Source: Authors' analysis of *Juvenile Residential Facility Census 2010* [machine-readable data file].

State-operated facilities made up just 21% of all facilities, and they accounted for 42% of facilities holding more than 200 residents. Private facilities constituted 49% of all facilities, and they accounted for 69% of facilities holding 10 or fewer residents.

Facility crowding affected a substantial proportion of youth in custody

Many juvenile offenders were in facilities with more residents than standard beds

Facilities reported both the number of standard beds and the number of makeshift beds they had on the census date. Occupancy rates provide the broadest assessment of the adequacy of living space. Although occupancy rate standards have not been established, as a facility's occupancy surpasses 100%, operational functioning may be compromised.

Crowding occurs when the number of residents occupying all or part of a facility exceeds some predetermined limit based on square footage, utility use, or even fire codes. Although it is an imperfect measure of crowding, comparing the number of residents to the number of standard beds gives a sense of the crowding problem in a facility. Even without relying on makeshift beds, a facility may be crowded. For example, using standard beds in an infirmary for youth who are not sick or beds in seclusion for youth who have not committed infractions may indicate crowding problems.

Twenty percent (20%) of facilities said that the number of residents they held on the 2010 census date put them at or over the capacity of their standard beds or that they relied on some makeshift beds. These facilities held 12,001 residents, the vast majority of whom were offenders younger than 21. Thus, 15% of all residents held on the census date and 16% of offenders younger than 21 were held in facilities operating at or above their standard bed capacity. In comparison, such facilities held 21% of all residents in 2008, and they held 40% in 2000. In 2010, 2% of facilities reported being over capacity (having fewer standard beds than they had residents or relying on makeshift beds). These facilities held 3% of juvenile offenders.

Compared with other types of facilities, public training schools, detention centers, and reception/diagnostic centers were more likely to be over their standard bed capacity

Facility type	Percentage of facilities at their standard bed capacity			Percentage of facilities over their standard bed capacity		
	Total	Public	Private	Total	Public	Private
Total	18%	12%	25%	2%	3%	0%
Detention center	10	9	13	4	4	2
Shelter	10	8	11	0	0	0
Reception/diagnostic center	11	8	18	3	4	0
Group home	30	16	33	0	1	0
Ranch/wilderness camp	15	19	11	0	0	0
Training school	11	9	29	4	5	0
Residential treatment center	22	17	24	1	2	0

The largest facilities were the most likely to be crowded

Facility size	Number of facilities	Percentage of facilities under, at, or over their standard bed capacity			Mean number of makeshift beds at facilities over capacity
		<100%	100%	>100%	
Total facilities	2,111	80%	18%	2%	6
1–10 residents	676	77	22	1	2
11–20 residents	481	80	19	1	2
21–50 residents	563	79	18	2	3
51–100 residents	243	86	11	4	4
101–200 residents	108	83	10	6	17
201+ residents	40	93	5	3	16

Note: A single bed is counted as one standard bed, and a bunk bed is counted as two standard beds. Makeshift beds (e.g., cots, roll-out beds, mattresses, and sofas) are not counted as standard beds. Facilities are counted as over capacity if they reported more residents than standard beds or if they reported any occupied makeshift beds. Facilities could select more than one facility type.

Source: Authors' analysis of *Juvenile Residential Facility Census 2010* [machine-readable data file].

43 states held fewer juvenile offenders in 2010 than in 2008

Overall, the juvenile offender custody population dropped 18% from 2008 to 2010. States with declines held an average of 19% fewer juvenile offenders on the census date in 2010 than in 2008—ranging from 46% in Vermont to 3% in Arizona.

Among the seven states that had more juveniles in residential placement in 2010 than in 2008, the average growth was 27%. The number of juvenile offenders at facilities in North Dakota more than doubled (127%). Five states had increases of 13% or less (Alaska, District of Columbia, Maryland, Missouri, and Montana), and New Mexico reported an increase of 23%. Rhode Island reported virtually no change in their custody population between 2008 and 2010.

Public facilities were more likely than private facilities to be crowded

Among publicly operated facilities, 3% exceeded standard bed capacity or had residents occupying makeshift beds on the 2010 census date. For privately operated facilities, the proportion was less than 1%. However, a larger proportion of private facilities (25%) compared to public facilities (12%) said they were operating at 100% capacity.

State-operated public facilities had a slightly greater proportion of facilities that exceeded capacity (4%) than did locally operated facilities (3%).

Facility operation	Percentage of facilities at or over their standard bed capacity		
	≥100%	100%	>100%
Total	20%	18%	2%
Public	15	12	3
State	18	13	4
Local	13	10	3
Private	25	25	0

Note: Detail may not add to totals because of rounding.

Use of makeshift beds varied widely

About 40 facilities reported having occupied makeshift beds, averaging 6 such beds per facility. Many facilities rely on makeshift beds, whereas many others operate well below standard bed capacity. On average, there were three unoccupied standard beds per facility. This average masks a wide range: 1 facility with 122 residents had 72 standard beds and 50 residents without standard beds; another facility with 432 standard beds had 253 residents, leaving 179 unoccupied beds.

Nationwide, 422 juvenile facilities (20%) were at or over standard capacity or relied on makeshift beds

State	Total facilities	Number of facilities under, at, or over capacity			Percentage of juvenile offenders in facilities at or over capacity		State	Total facilities	Number of facilities under, at, or over capacity			Percentage of juvenile offenders in facilities at or over capacity	
		<100%	100%	>100%	100%	>100%			<100%	100%	>100%	100%	>100%
U.S. total	2,111	1,689	383	39	13%	3%	Missouri	64	42	17	5	27%	13%
Alabama	49	44	5	0	5	0	Montana	15	13	2	0	6	0
Alaska	19	18	1	0	3	0	Nebraska	12	9	1	2	0	17
Arizona	40	33	6	1	8	1	Nevada	22	14	6	2	12	28
Arkansas	33	24	8	1	31	6	New Hampshire	7	5	2	0	11	0
California	202	138	62	2	16	1	New Jersey	39	35	4	0	3	0
Colorado	45	40	3	2	4	13	New Mexico	22	20	1	1	16	10
Connecticut	10	10	0	0	0	0	New York	126	96	29	1	9	0
Delaware	7	6	1	0	8	0	North Carolina	41	33	7	1	11	1
Dist. of Columbia	9	6	1	2	5	78	North Dakota	14	10	4	0	29	0
Florida	97	73	22	2	18	1	Ohio	77	59	13	5	20	10
Georgia	33	28	1	4	2	16	Oklahoma	36	20	16	0	27	0
Hawaii	5	5	0	0	0	0	Oregon	44	35	9	0	22	0
Idaho	20	20	0	0	0	0	Pennsylvania	131	98	32	1	21	3
Illinois	40	39	1	0	1	0	Rhode Island	11	4	7	0	29	0
Indiana	70	60	9	1	8	1	South Carolina	21	18	3	0	5	0
Iowa	63	52	11	0	13	0	South Dakota	24	20	4	0	20	0
Kansas	34	22	10	2	11	10	Tennessee	38	30	7	1	8	3
Kentucky	33	27	6	0	14	0	Texas	97	89	6	2	2	5
Louisiana	34	27	6	1	31	2	Utah	28	22	6	0	20	0
Maine	4	4	0	0	0	0	Vermont	3	3	0	0	0	0
Maryland	30	21	9	0	39	0	Virginia	52	48	3	1	5	1
Massachusetts	52	44	8	0	16	0	Washington	34	29	5	0	14	0
Michigan	63	59	4	0	4	0	West Virginia	26	21	5	0	23	0
Minnesota	55	49	6	0	13	0	Wisconsin	66	54	12	0	11	0
Mississippi	17	16	1	0	1	0	Wyoming	16	14	2	0	5	0

Note: A single bed is counted as one standard bed, and a bunk bed is counted as two standard beds. Makeshift beds (e.g., cots, roll-out beds, mattresses, and sofas) are not counted as standard beds. Facilities are counted as over capacity if they reported more residents than standard beds or if they reported any occupied makeshift beds. Facilities could select more than one facility type. "State" is the state where the facility is located. Offenders sent to out-of-state facilities are counted in the state where the facility is located, not the state where they committed their offense.

Source: Authors' analysis of *Juvenile Residential Facility Census 2010* [machine-readable data file].

Most juvenile offenders were evaluated for educational needs and attended school while held in facilities

Facilities that screened all youth for educational needs held 86% of the offenders in custody

As part of the information collected on educational services, the JRFC questionnaire asked facilities about their procedures regarding educational screening.

In 2010, 87% of facilities that reported educational screening information said that they evaluated all youth for grade level and educational needs. An additional 5% evaluated some youth. Only 9% did not evaluate any youth for educational needs.

Of the 91 facilities in 2010 that screened some but not all youth, 73% evaluated youth whom staff identified as needing an assessment, 61% evaluated youth with known educational problems, 55% evaluated youth for whom no educational record was available, and 16% evaluated youth who came directly from home rather than from another facility.

In 2010, those facilities that screened all youth held 86% of the juvenile offenders in custody. An additional 3% of juvenile offenders in 2010 were in facilities that screened some youth.

Most facilities used previous academic records to evaluate educational needs

The vast majority of facilities (89%) that screened some or all youth for grade level and educational needs used previous academic records. Some facilities also administered written tests (67%) or conducted an education-related interview with an education specialist (61%), intake counselor (38%), or guidance counselor (25%).

The smallest facilities were the least likely to evaluate all youth for grade level

| Education screening | Facility size based on residential population | | | | | | |
	Total	1–10	11–20	21–50	51–100	101–200	201+
Total facilities	2,111	676	481	563	243	108	40
Facilities reporting	1,959	624	456	519	226	99	35
All reporting facilities	100%	100%	100%	100%	100%	100%	100%
All youth screened	87	75	89	94	94	96	100
Some youth screened	5	8	4	3	4	3	0
No youth screened	9	18	7	3	3	1	0

■ The largest facilities evaluated 100% of youth for grade level in 2010.

Note: Column percentages may not add up to 100% due to rounding.

Source: Authors' analysis of *Juvenile Residential Facility Census 2010* [machine-readable data file].

Most facilities evaluated youth for grade level between 24 hours and 7 days after arrival

| When youth are evaluated for educational needs | Number of juvenile facilities | | | As a percentage of facilities that evaluated youth for grade level | | |
	All facilities	All youth evaluated	Some youth evaluated	Facilities that evaluated	All youth evaluated	Some youth evaluated
Total facilities	2,111	1,701	91	100%	95%	5%
Less than 24 hours	385	378	7	21	21	0
24 hours to 7 days	1,383	1,334	49	77	74	3
7 or more days	177	151	26	10	8	1
Other	73	55	18	4	3	1
No youth evaluated (or not reported)	319	–	–	–	–	–

Note: Facilities sum to more than 2,111 because they could select more than one time period.

Source: Authors' analysis of *Juvenile Residential Facility Census 2010* [machine-readable data file].

Most facilities reported that youth in their facility attended school

Ninety-two percent (92%) of facilities reported that at least some youth in their facility attended school either inside or outside the facility. Facilities reporting that all youth attended school (73% of facilities) accounted for 72% of the juvenile offender population in residential placement. Ranch/wilderness camps were the least likely to report that all youth attended school (63%) and the most likely to report that no youth attended school (15%). Facilities with 11–20 residents and 21–50 residents were most likely to report that all youth attended school (77% each), while facilities with 201+ residents were least likely (58%) to have all youth attend

Ranch/wilderness camps and small facilities were the least likely to report that youth in their facility attended school

Facility type	Total	Percentage of facilities with youth attending school		
		All youth	Some youth	No youth
Total facilities	100%	73%	19%	8%
Detention center	100	79	16	4
Shelter	100	72	23	5
Reception/diagnostic center	100	75	19	6
Group home	100	65	25	10
Ranch/wilderness camp	100	63	22	15
Training school	100	70	22	7
Residential treatment center	100	75	17	9
Facility size				
1–10 residents	100%	69%	22%	9%
11–20 residents	100	77	18	6
21–50 residents	100	77	15	8
51–100 residents	100	75	17	7
101–200 residents	100	68	24	8
201+ residents	100	58	30	13

Note: Row percentages may not add up to 100% due to rounding.

Source: Authors' analysis of *Juvenile Residential Facility Census 2010* [machine-readable data file].

Most facilities provided middle and high school-level education

Education level	Facility type							
	All facilities	Detention center	Shelter	Reception/ diagnostic center	Group home	Ranch/ wilderness camp	Training school	Residential treatment center
Elementary level	50%	73%	61%	49%	30%	49%	45%	43%
Middle school	84	93	93	93	79	78	82	85
High school	91	93	93	94	90	85	93	91
Special education	82	83	80	89	79	82	88	83
GED preparation	71	68	73	71	75	59	79	74
GED testing	51	36	50	56	60	47	82	56
Post-high school	31	18	19	40	40	29	63	34
Vocational/technical	38	17	26	50	48	50	74	49
Life skills training	62	55	58	65	64	60	70	68

Source: Authors' analysis of *Juvenile Residential Facility Census 2010* [machine-readable data file].

school. Facilities reporting that no youth attended school (8%) accounted for 9% of all juvenile offenders in residential placement.

Facilities offered a variety of educational services

Facilities that provided both middle and high school-level education housed 83% of all juvenile offenders. Ninety-one percent (91%) of all facilities provided high school-level education, and 84% provided middle school-level education. Most facilities also reported offering special education services (82%) and GED preparation (71%). A much smaller percentage of facilities provided vocational or technical education (38%) and post-high school education (31%).

In 2010, facilities were asked if they communicated information regarding the education status, services, and/or needs to the young person's new placement or residence; 86% of facilities said that they did. Most of these (87%) said that they communicated education status information for all youth departing the facility.

Most facilities reported screening youth for substance abuse problems

Facilities that screened all youth held 66% of the juvenile offenders in custody

In 2010, 70% of facilities that reported substance abuse evaluation information said that they evaluated all youth, 17% said that they evaluated some youth, and 13% did not evaluate any youth.

Of the 330 facilities that evaluated some but not all youth, 85% evaluated youth that the court or a probation officer identified as potentially having substance abuse problems, 74% evaluated youth that facility staff identified as potentially having substance abuse problems, and 57% evaluated youth charged with or adjudicated for a drug- or alcohol-related offense.

Those facilities that screened all youth held 66% of the juvenile offenders in custody. An additional 16% of juvenile offenders were in facilities that screened some youth.

The most common form of evaluation was a series of staff-administered questions

The majority of facilities (74%) that evaluated some or all youth for substance abuse problems had staff administer a series of questions that ask about substance use and abuse, 59% evaluated youth by visual observation, 52% evaluated youth by using a self-report checklist inventory that asks about substance use and abuse, and 41% said they used a standardized self-report instrument such as the Substance Abuse Subtle Screening Inventory.

Both the smallest and the largest facilities were the least likely to evaluate all youth for substance abuse problems

Substance abuse screening	Facility size based on residential population						
	Total	1–10	11–20	21–50	51–100	101–200	201+
Total facilities	2,111	676	481	563	243	108	40
Facilities reporting	1,959	624	456	519	226	99	35
All reporting facilities	100%	100%	100%	100%	100%	100%	100%
All youth screened	70	65	74	72	71	73	66
Some youth screened	17	19	14	15	18	22	20
No youth screened	13	16	12	12	11	5	14

Note: Column percentages may not add up to 100% due to rounding.

Source: Authors' analysis of *Juvenile Residential Facility Census 2010* [machine-readable data file].

More than half of facilities reported evaluating youth for substance abuse within their first day at the facility

When youth are evaluated for substance abuse	Number of juvenile facilities			As a percentage of facilities that evaluated youth for substance abuse		
	All facilities	All youth evaluated	Some youth evaluated	Facilities that evaluated	All youth evaluated	Some youth evaluated
Total facilities	2,111	1,376	330	100%	81%	19%
Less than 24 hours	1,023	937	86	60	55	5
24 hours to 7 days	652	525	127	38	31	7
7 or more days	166	103	63	10	6	4
Other	174	67	107	10	4	6
No youth evaluated (or not reported)	405	–	–	–	–	–

Note: Facilities sum to more than 2,111 because they were able to select more than one time period.

Source: Authors' analysis of *Juvenile Residential Facility Census 2010* [machine-readable data file].

Drug testing was a routine procedure in most facilities in 2010

As part of the information collected on substance abuse services, JRFC asked facilities if they required any youth to undergo drug testing after they arrived at the facility. The majority of facilities (73%) reported that they required at least some youth to undergo drug testing. Of facilities that reported testing all or some youth, the reason for testing was most commonly due to a request from the court or probation officer (62% for facilities that tested all youth, 72% for facilities that tested youth suspected of recent drug or alcohol use, and 69% for facilities that tested youth with substance abuse problems).

Circumstances of testing	Percentage of facilities
All youth	
After initial arrival	26%
At each reentry	23
Randomly	31
When drug use is suspected or drug is present	52
At the request of the court or probation officer	62
Youth suspected of recent drug/alcohol use	
After initial arrival	34%
At each reentry	26
Randomly	33
When drug use is suspected or drug is present	59
At the request of the court or probation officer	72
Youth with substance abuse problems	
After initial arrival	27%
At each reentry	26
Randomly	35
When drug use is suspected or drug is present	53
At the request of the court or probation officer	69

In 2010, JRFC asked facilities if they communicated information regarding the substance abuse status, services, and/or needs to the young person's new placement or residence; 58% of facilities said that they did. Of these facilities, many (69%) said that they communicated substance abuse status information for all youth departing the facility.

Substance abuse education was the most common service provided at all reporting facilities

Substance abuse service	Facility size based on residential population						
	Total	1–10	11–20	21–50	51–100	101–200	201+
Total facilities	2,111	676	481	563	243	108	40
Facilities reporting	1,567	490	364	420	176	88	29
Substance abuse education	96%	95%	98%	96%	98%	94%	100%
Case manager to oversee treatment	49	44	45	50	58	60	59
Treatment plan for substance abuse	74	75	69	72	76	83	86
Special living units	10	6	3	7	21	38	55
None of above services provided	1	1	1	1	1	0	0

■ Of the facilities holding more than 200 residents that reported providing substance abuse services, all provided substance abuse education and were more likely than smaller facilities to have special living units in which all young persons have substance abuse offenses and/or problems.

Source: Authors' analysis of *Juvenile Residential Facility Census 2010* [machine-readable data file].

The majority of facilities that provided substance abuse counseling or therapy were most likely to provide services on an individual basis

Service provided	Facility type							
	Total	Detention center	Shelter	Reception/ diagnostic center	Group home	Ranch/ wilderness camp	Training school	Residential treatment center
Total facilities	2,111	705	137	72	528	68	188	763
Facilities reporting counseling	1,066	252	66	28	310	33	114	460
Individual	91%	89%	95%	93%	92%	82%	89%	92%
Group	85	78	74	89	83	91	94	88
Family	48	36	45	43	55	39	40	54
Facilities reporting therapy	1,347	325	87	39	414	40	144	561
Individual	96%	94%	98%	97%	96%	88%	97%	96%
Group	86	77	85	100	84	98	91	92
Family	50	44	56	46	51	38	46	56

■ In 2010, shelters were most likely to provide individual counseling and individual therapy.

■ Training schools were the most likely to provide group counseling, and 100% of reception/diagnostic centers reported providing group therapy.

■ Almost half of all facilities provided family counseling or family therapy.

Note: Counts (and row percentages) may sum to more than the total number of facilities because facilities could select more than one facility type.

Source: Authors' analysis of *Juvenile Residential Facility Census 2010* [machine-readable data file].

Half of juvenile offenders were in facilities where in-house mental health professionals assess all youth

In approximately 6 of 10 facilities, in-house mental health professionals evaluated all youth held

Facilities provided information about their procedures for evaluating youth's mental health needs. Among facilities that responded to mental health evaluation questions in 2010, 57% reported that they evaluated all youth for mental health needs, and 42% evaluated some but not all youth. Only 1% said that they did not evaluate any youth (either inside or outside the facility) during their stay.

In 2010, a greater proportion of privately operated than publicly operated facilities said that in-house mental health professionals evaluated all youth (79% vs. 49% of facilities reporting mental health evaluation information). However, in a greater proportion of public facilities than private facilities (51% vs. 21%), in-house mental health professionals evaluated some youth.

Evaluation by in-house mental health professional	Facility type	
	Public	Private
Total reporting facilities	889	695
All reporting facilities	100%	100%
All youth screened	49	79
Some youth screened	51	21

Facilities also identified themselves according to the type of treatment they provided (if any). Facilities that said they provided mental health treatment inside the facility were more likely than other facilities to have a mental health professional evaluate all youth (66% vs. 34% of

those reporting mental health evaluation information).

Evaluation by in-house mental health professional	Onsite mental health treatment?	
	Yes	No
Total reporting facilities	1,410	174
All reporting facilities	100%	100%
All youth screened	66	34
Some youth screened	34	66

The smallest facilities were most likely to have in-house mental health professionals evaluate all youth for mental health needs

In-house mental health evaluation	Facility size based on residential population						
	Total	1–10	11–20	21–50	51–100	101–200	201+
Total facilities	2,111	676	481	563	243	108	40
Facilities reporting	1,584	415	359	464	215	97	34
All reporting facilities	100%	100%	100%	100%	100%	100%	100%
All youth evaluated	62	66	61	59	64	64	59
Some youth evaluated	38	34	39	41	36	36	41

Source: Authors' analysis of *Juvenile Residential Facility Census 2010* [machine-readable data file].

Group homes and residential treatment centers were more likely than other types of facilities to have in-house mental health professionals evaluate all youth for mental health needs

In-house mental health evaluation	Facility type						
	Detention center	Shelter	Reception/ diagnostic center	Group home	Ranch/ wilderness camp	Training school	Residential treatment center
Total facilities	705	137	72	528	68	188	763
Facilities reporting	570	80	66	331	43	169	638
All reporting facilities	100%	100%	100%	100%	100%	100%	100%
All youth evaluated	34	40	71	79	56	74	77
Some youth evaluated	66	60	29	21	44	26	23

Source: Authors' analysis of *Juvenile Residential Facility Census 2010* [machine-readable data file].

In 2010, JRFC asked facilities if they communicated information regarding the mental health status, services, and/or needs to the young person's new placement or residence; 96% of facilities said that they did. Most of these (70%) said that they communicated mental health status information for all youth departing the facility.

The most common approach to in-house mental health evaluation was to screen all youth by the end of their first day or first week at the facility

When youth are evaluated for mental health needs	Number of juvenile facilities			As a percentage of facilities that evaluated youth in-house for mental health needs		
	All facilities	All youth evaluated	Some youth evaluated	Facilities that evaluated	All youth evaluated	Some youth evaluated
Total facilities reporting	1,584	989	595	100%	62%	38%
Less than 24 hours	614	455	159	39	29	10
24 hours to 7 days	620	456	164	39	29	10
7 or more days	101	53	48	6	3	3
Other	249	25	224	16	2	14

■ In 58% of facilities that reported using an in-house mental health professional to perform mental health evaluations, they evaluated all youth for mental health needs by the end of their first week in custody.

Note: Percentage detail may not add up to total due to rounding.

Source: Authors' analysis of *Juvenile Residential Facility Census 2010* [machine-readable data file].

Of facilities that reported using in-house mental health professionals to conduct mental health evaluations, 33% of juvenile offenders were in facilities that evaluated all youth on the day they arrived at the facility

When youth are evaluated for mental health needs	Number of juvenile offenders			As a percentage of juvenile offenders in facilities that provided in-house evaluation for mental health needs		
	All facilities	All youth evaluated	Some youth evaluated	Facilities that evaluated	All youth evaluated	Some youth evaluated
Total juvenile offenders residing in reporting facilities	55,469	33,594	21,875	100%	61%	39%
Less than 24 hours	25,815	18,168	7,647	47	33	14
24 hours to 7 days	18,726	12,890	5,836	34	23	11
7 or more days	2,693	1,479	1,214	5	3	2
Other	8,235	1,057	7,178	15	2	13

■ Facilities reporting that they evaluated all youth by the end of their first week held 56% of juvenile offenders who resided in facilities that reported using in-house mental health evaluation procedures.

Note: Percentage detail may not add up to total due to rounding.

Source: Authors' analysis of *Juvenile Residential Facility Census 2010* [machine-readable data file].

Most juvenile offenders were held in facilities that evaluate all youth for suicide risk on their first day

Facilities that screened all youth for suicide risk held 93% of the juvenile offenders in custody

As part of the information collected on mental health services, the JRFC questionnaire asks facilities about their procedures regarding screening youth for suicide risk.

In 2010, 89% of facilities that reported information on suicide screening said that they evaluated all youth for suicide risk.

An additional 3% said that they evaluated some youth. Some facilities (7%) said that they did not evaluate any youth for suicide risk.

In 2010, a larger proportion of public than private facilities said that they evaluated all youth for suicide risk (94% vs. 84%).

In 2010, among facilities that reported suicide screening information, those that screened all youth for suicide risk held 93% of juvenile offenders who were in residential placement—up from 81% in 2002 and 78% in 2000. An additional 3% of juvenile offenders in 2010 were in facilities that screened some youth.

Suicide screening	2000	2010
Total juvenile offenders	110,284	66,322
Offenders in reporting facilities	104,956	60,678
Total offenders	100%	100%
All youth screened	78	93
Some youth screened	16	3
No youth screened	6	5

Note: Detail may not total 100% because of rounding.

Some facilities used trained counselors or professional mental health staff to conduct suicide screening

Less than half (44%) of facilities that screened some or all youth for suicide risk reported that mental health professionals with at least a master's degree in psychology or social work conducted the screenings. One-third (33%) used neither mental health professionals nor counselors whom a mental health professional had trained to conduct suicide screenings.

Facilities reported on the screening methods used to determine suicide risk. Facilities could choose more than one method. Of facilities that conducted suicide risk screening, the majority (76%) reported that they incorporated 1 or more questions about suicide in the medical history or intake process to screen youth; 41% used a form their facility designed, and 21% used a form or questions that a county or state juvenile justice system designed to assess suicide risk. Approximately 4 in 10 facilities (39%) reported using the Massachusetts Youth Screening Instrument (MAYSI); 32% reported using

Suicide screening was common across facilities of all sizes

Suicide screening	Facility size based on residential population						
	Total	1–10	11–20	21–50	51–100	101–200	201+
Total facilities	2,111	676	481	563	243	108	40
Facilities reporting	1,959	624	456	519	226	99	35
All reporting facilities	100%	100%	100%	100%	100%	100%	100%
All youth screened	89	82	93	93	93	93	94
Some youth screened	3	6	1	3	2	4	3
No youth screened	7	12	6	4	5	3	3

Note: Column percentages may not add up to 100% due to rounding.

Source: Authors' analysis of *Juvenile Residential Facility Census 2010* [machine-readable data file].

Ranch/wilderness camps and group homes were the least likely to screen youth for suicide risk

Suicide screening	Facility type						
	Detention center	Shelter	Reception/ diagnostic center	Group home	Ranch/ wilderness camp	Training school	Residential treatment center
Total facilities	705	137	72	528	68	188	763
Facilities reporting	679	132	70	479	58	174	698
All reporting facilities	100%	100%	100%	100%	100%	100%	100%
All youth screened	97	88	93	76	72	97	92
Some youth screened	1	2	4	9	5	2	3
No youth screened	2	10	3	15	22	1	6

Note: Column percentages may not add up to 100% due to rounding.

Source: Authors' analysis of *Juvenile Residential Facility Census 2010* [machine-readable data file].

the MAYSI full form, and 7% used the MAYSI suicide/depression module. Very few facilities (1%) used the Voice Diagnostic Interview Schedule for Children.

Of facilities that reported screening youth for suicide risk, 86% reassessed youth at some point during their stay. Most facilities (88%) reported rescreening on a case-by-case basis or as necessary. An additional 33% of facilities also reported that rescreening occurred systematically and was based on a variety of factors (e.g., length of stay, facility events, or negative life events). Less than 1% of facilities did not reassess youth to determine suicide risk.

All facilities used some type of preventive measure once they determined a youth was at risk for suicide

Facilities that reported suicide screening information were asked a series of questions related to preventive measures taken for youth determined to be at risk for suicide. Of these facilities, 65% reported placing at-risk youth in sleeping or observation rooms that are locked or under staff security. Aside from using sleeping or observation rooms, equal proportions of facilities (83%) reported using line-of-sight supervision and removing personal items that could be used to attempt suicide, and approximately 7 in 10 facilities (71%) reported using one-on-one or arm's-length supervision. More than 4 in 10 facilities (42%) reported using special clothing to prevent suicide attempts, and 33% reported removing the youth from the general population. Twenty-one percent (21%) of facilities used restraints to prevent suicide attempts, and 18% of facilities used special clothing to identify youth at risk for suicide.

In 2010, the majority (91%) of juvenile offenders in facilities that screened for suicide risk were in facilities that conducted suicide screenings on all youth on the day they arrived

| Suicide screening | Total | When suicide risk screening occurs | | | | |
		Less than 24 hours	24 hours to 7 days	7 days or more	Other	Never or not reported
Number of facilities:						
All	2,111	1,602	162	13	44	290
All youth screened	1,753	1,563	147	11	32	–
Some youth screened	68	39	15	2	12	–
Percentage of facilities that screened:						
Total	100%	88%	9%	1%	2%	–
All youth screened	96	86	8	1	2	–
Some youth screened	4	2	1	0	1	–
Number of juvenile offenders:						
In all facilities	66,322	53,067	3,125	178	1,469	8,483
In facilities that screened all youth	56,316	52,438	2,914	166	798	–
In facilities that screened some youth	1,523	629	211	12	671	–
Percentage of juvenile offenders:						
In facilities that screened	100%	92%	5%	0%	3%	–
In facilities that screened all youth	97	91	5	0	1	–
In facilities that screened some youth	3	1	0	0	1	–

■ More than 9 in 10 facilities (94%) that reported screening for suicide risk said they screened all youth by the end of the first week of their stay at the facility. A large portion (86%) said they screened all youth on their first day at the facility. These facilities accounted for 91% of juvenile offenders held in facilities that conducted suicide screenings.

■ Very few facilities that reported screening for suicide risk reported that they conducted the screenings at some point other than within the first week of a youth's stay (3%). Facilities that conducted screenings within other time limits gave varying responses. For example, some facilities reported that screenings occurred as needed or as deemed necessary. Some reported that screenings were court ordered. Other facilities reported that screenings occurred when the youth indicated suicidal behavior or expressed suicidal thoughts. A small number of facilities indicated that screenings occurred before the youth was admitted.

Note: Percentage detail may not add up to total due to rounding.

Source: Authors' analysis of *Juvenile Residential Facility Census 2010* [machine-readable data file].

JRFC asks facilities about certain activities that may have occurred in the month before the census date

In addition to information gathered on the census date, JRFC collects data on the following questions for the 30-day period of September 2010:

- Were there any unauthorized departures of any young persons who were assigned beds at this facility?

- Were any young persons assigned beds at this facility transported to a hospital emergency room by facility staff, transportation staff, or by an ambulance?

- Were any of the young persons assigned beds here restrained by facility staff with a mechanical restraint?

- Were any of the young persons assigned beds here locked for more than 4 hours alone in an isolation, seclusion, or sleeping room to regain control of their unruly behavior?

One fifth of facilities (20%) reported unauthorized departures in the month before the census date

Facility type	Number of facilities		Percentage of reporting facilities with unauthorized departures
	Total	Reporting	
Total facilities	2,111	1,959	20%
Detention center	705	679	3
Shelter	137	132	38
Reception/diagnostic center	72	70	21
Group home	528	479	35
Ranch/wilderness camp	68	58	24
Training school	188	174	9
Residential treatment center	763	698	26

- Shelters and group homes were most likely to report one or more unauthorized departures.

Note: Detail may sum to more than the totals because facilities could select more than one facility type.

Source: Authors' analysis of *Juvenile Residential Facility Census 2010* [machine-readable data file].

Sports-related injuries were the most common reason for emergency room visits in the previous month

Reason for ER visit	Percentage of facilities
Total	33%
Injury	
Sports-related	42
Work/chore-related	2
Interpersonal conflict (between residents)	21
Interpersonal conflict (by nonresident)	4
Illness	37
Pregnancy	
Complications	5
Labor and delivery	1
Suicide attempt	6
Non-emergency	
No other health professional available	13
No doctor's appointment could be obtained	10
Other	25

Note: Percentages are based on facilities that reported emergency room information (32 of 2,111 facilities [1%] did not report).

Source: Authors' analysis of *Juvenile Residential Facility Census 2010* [machine-readable data file].

Approximately 1 in 4 facilities reported using mechanical restraints; 1 in 5 reported locking youth in some type of isolation

Facility type	Percentage of reporting facilities	
	Used mechanical restraints	Locked youth in room for 4 or more hours
Total facilities	23%	22%
Detention center	41	47
Shelter	4	4
Reception/diagnostic center	47	32
Group home	1	1
Ranch/wilderness camp	28	12
Training school	72	47
Residential treatment center	14	10

- Training schools were the most likely type of facility to use mechanical restraints (i.e., handcuffs, leg cuffs, waist bands, leather straps, restraining chairs, strait jackets, or other mechanical devices) in the previous month. Detention centers and training schools were the most likely to lock a youth alone in some type of seclusion for 4 or more hours to regain control of their unruly behavior.

- Group homes were the facility type least likely to use either of these measures.

Note: Percentages are based on 1,958 facilities that reported mechanical restraints information and locked isolation information, of a total 2,111 facilities.

Source: Authors' analysis of *Juvenile Residential Facility Census 2010* [machine-readable data file].

Facilities reported 11 deaths of juvenile offenders in custody over 12 months—5 were suicides

Juvenile offenders rarely died in custody

Juvenile facilities holding juvenile offenders reported that 11 youth died while in the legal custody of the facility between October 1, 2009, and September 30, 2010. Each death occurred at a different facility.

Routine collection of national data on deaths of juveniles in custody began with the 1988/89 Children in Custody (CIC) Census of Public and Private Juvenile Detention, Correctional, and Shelter Facilities. Accidents or suicides have usually been the leading cause of death. Over the years 1988–1994 (CIC data reporting years), there were an average of 46 deaths reported nationally per year, including an annual average of 18 suicides. Over the years 2000–2010 (JRFC data reporting years), those averages dropped to 20 deaths overall and 8 suicides. In 2006, the number of suicides that occurred at residential facilities (four) was the lowest since OJJDP first started collecting data from JRFC in 2000. There were five suicides in 2010.

Detention centers and residential treatment centers reported equal numbers of deaths in 2010 (four each). Detention centers accounted for two deaths due to illness or natural causes, one suicide, and one death as a result of an accident. Residential treatment centers accounted for two deaths as the result of illness or natural causes, one suicide, and one death as the result of an unknown cause. Group homes accounted for 2 of the 11 deaths; both were suicides. Training schools accounted for 1 of the 11 deaths—a suicide.

During the 12 months prior to the census, suicides were the most commonly reported cause of death in custody

Cause of death	Total	Inside the facility			Outside the facility		
		All	Public	Private	All	Public	Private
Total	11	6	5	1	5	1	4
Suicide	5	3	3	0	2	0	2
Illness/natural	4	1	1	0	3	1	2
Accident	1	1	1	0	0	0	0
Homicide	0	0	0	0	0	0	0
Other/unknown	1	1	0	1	0	0	0

■ None of the deaths from illness were AIDS related.

Notes: Data are reported deaths of youth in custody from October 1, 2009, through September 30, 2010.

Source: Authors' analysis of *Juvenile Residential Facility Census 2010* [machine-readable data file].

In 2010, the death rate was generally higher for private facilities than for public facilities

Cause of death	Deaths per 10,000 juveniles held on the census date, October 27, 2010		
	Total	Public facility	Private facility
Total	1.6	1.3	2.5
Suicide	0.7	0.6	1.0
Illness/natural	0.6	0.4	1.0
Accident	0.1	0.2	0.0
Homicide	0.0	0.0	0.0
Other	0.1	0.0	0.5

Type of facility	Deaths per 10,000 juveniles held on the census date, October 27, 2010		
	Total	Public facility	Private facility
Detention center	1.4	1.6	0.0
Training school	0.6	0.7	0.0
Group home	3.1	8.4	1.9
Residential treatment center	1.6	0.0	3.1

■ The death rate in 2010 (1.6) was substantially lower than that in 2000 (2.8). There were 30 reported deaths of youth in custody in 2000; accidents were the most commonly reported cause. In 2010, suicides were the most commonly reported cause (followed closely by illness/natural causes).

Note: Data are reported deaths of youth in custody from October 1, 2009, through September 30, 2010.

Source: Authors' analysis of *Juvenile Residential Facility Census 2010* [machine-readable data file].

Of the total deaths in custody (11), 5 involved white non-Hispanic males and 4 involved black non-Hispanic males

Race/ethnicity	Total		Suicide		Illness/natural		Accident		Homicide		Other	
	Male	Female	Male	Female	Male	Female	Male	Female	Male	Female	Male	Female
Total	11	0	5	0	4	0	1	0	0	0	1	0
White non-Hispanic	5	0	3	0	1	0	0	0	0	0	1	0
Black non-Hispanic	4	0	0	0	3	0	1	0	0	0	0	0
American Indian/Alaska Native	1	0	1	0	0	0	0	0	0	0	0	0
Asian/Pacific Islander	0	0	0	0	0	0	0	0	0	0	0	0
Hispanic	0	0	0	0	0	0	0	0	0	0	0	0
Other race/ethnicity	1	0	1	0	0	0	0	0	0	0	0	0

Note: Data are reported deaths of youth in custody from October 1, 2009, through September 30, 2010.

Source: Authors' analysis of *Juvenile Residential Facility Census 2010* [machine-readable data file].

Generally, suicides did not occur in the first days of a youth's stay

One suicide occurred 2 days after the youth was admitted to the facility, one occurred 4 weeks after admission, one occurred 23 weeks after admission, and the remaining two suicides occurred just over 1 year after admission. The least number of days since admission for deaths was the suicide that occurred 2 days after admission, and the greatest number of days was a death as a result of an illness after the youth had been in custody for 514 days (about a year and a half). The overall median number of days since admission for deaths of juveniles in custody was 159.

JRFC asks facilities about deaths of young persons at locations inside and/or outside the facility

During the year between October 1, 2009, and September 30, 2010, did ANY young persons die while assigned to a bed at this facility at a location either INSIDE or OUTSIDE of this facility?

If yes, how many young persons died while assigned beds at this facility during the year between October 1, 2009, and September 30, 2010?

What was the cause of death?

■ Illness/natural causes (excluding AIDS)

■ Injury suffered prior to placement here

■ AIDS

■ Suicide

■ Homicide by another resident

■ Homicide by nonresident(s)

■ Accidental death

■ Other (specify)

What was the location of death, age, sex, race, date of admission to the facility, and date of death for each young person who died while assigned a bed at this facility?

The Juvenile Residential Facility Census includes data submitted by tribal facilities

OJJDP worked with the Bureau of Indian Affairs (BIA) to ensure a greater representation of tribal facilities in the CJRP and JRFC data collections. As a result, the 2010 JRFC collected data from 19 tribal facilities (up from 8 in 2008). The tribal facilities were in Arizona, Colorado, Michigan, Minnesota, Mississippi, Montana, New Mexico, North Dakota, Oklahoma, and South Dakota and held 235 juvenile offenders (up from 101 in 2008).

Of the reporting tribal facilities, the tribe owned and operated 10, the federal government owned and operated 3, the tribed owned and the federal government operated 1, and the federal government

owned and the tribe operated 1. The tribe owned but an "other" organization (BIA and PL 93–638 contract) operated two facilities. One facility did not report ownership information but was privately operated. The remaining facility did not report ownership or operation information.

All 19 tribal facilities identified themselves as detention centers. One facility also identified itself as an "other" type of facility. They held from 28 to 109 residents, with 42% of facilities holding between 11 and 20 residents. On the census day, almost all facilities (17) were operating at less than their standard bed

capacity, one was operating at capacity, and one exceeded capacity. Standard bed capacities ranged from 13 to 186; only 2 facilities had more than 100 beds.

Seventeen of the 19 tribal facilities reported locking youth in their sleeping rooms. Among tribal facilities that locked youth in their rooms, most (16 facilities) did so at night, 11 did so when youth were out of control, 10 did so when youth were in their sleeping rooms, 9 did so during shift changes, and 7 did so when a youth was considered suicidal. Three facilities locked youth in their rooms all day, and 1 facility reported rarely locking youth in their rooms.

Resources

OJJDP's online Statistical Briefing Book (SBB) offers access to a wealth of information about juvenile crime and victimization and about youth involved in the juvenile justice system. Visit the "Juveniles in Corrections" section of the SBB at ojjdp.gov/ojstatbb/corrections/faqs.asp for the latest information about juveniles in corrections. The **Census of Juveniles in Residential Placement Databook** contains a large set of predefined tables detailing the characteristics of juvenile offenders in residential placement facilities. **Easy Access to the Census of Juveniles in Residential Placement** is a data analysis tool that gives users quick access to national data on the characteristics of youth held in residential placement facilities.

Data sources

Office of Juvenile Justice and Delinquency Prevention. 2001, 2003, 2005, 2007, 2009, and 2011. Juvenile Residential Facility Census for the years 2000, 2002, 2004, 2006, 2008, and 2010 [machine-readable data files]. Washington, DC: U.S. Census Bureau (producer).

This bulletin was prepared under cooperative agreement number 2010–MU–FX–K058 from the Office of Juvenile Justice and Delinquency Prevention (OJJDP), U.S. Department of Justice.

Points of view or opinions expressed in this document are those of the authors and do not necessarily represent the official position or policies of OJJDP or the U.S. Department of Justice.

Acknowledgments

This bulletin was written by Sarah Hockenberry, Research Associate, and Anthony Sladky, Senior Computer Programmer, with assistance from Melissa Sickmund, Director at the National Center for Juvenile Justice, with funds provided by OJJDP to support the National Juvenile Justice Data Analysis Project.

The Office of Juvenile Justice and Delinquency Prevention is a component of the Office of Justice Programs, which also includes the Bureau of Justice Assistance; the Bureau of Justice Statistics; the National Institute of Justice; the Office for Victims of Crime; and the Office of Sex Offender Sentencing, Monitoring, Apprehending, Registering, and Tracking.